A Wasteland of Words

Justicelee Auman

BookLeaf
Publishing

India | USA | UK

Presentation by *BookLeaf Publishing*

Web: www.bookleafpub.com

E-mail: info@bookleafpub.com

ISBN: 9789360947170

First edition 2024

ACKNOWLEDGEMENT

A thank you to everyone. I wouldn't be me without all of you.

Adapt

With each new hurdle, we must find a way,
To change, to thrive, come whatever may,
In the book of life, we read our line,
Adapting, growing, knowing we'll be fine,

When trials are faced, and things look bad,
We find strength we didn't know we had,
In ebb and flow, resilience resides,
Forever moving, like the tides,

Like trees in the wind, we sway,
Learning what to do and what to say,
We learn to expand, not to forsake,
Like wood that will bend, but never break.

Conceited

I spent the last two weeks just spinning,
I spent the last two weeks just grinning,
The last two weeks I've caught myself singing,
The last two weeks I've been constantly
winning,

I never thought that such self-deprecation,
Could lead me to this much self-reclamation,
Now, so easy for auto-abjuration,
Like every breath is a celebration,

After sewing my torn seam,
I hold myself in high esteem,
I perceive things unlike they seem,
Like my whole life is a daydream,

A feeling as unnerving as inevitability itself,
Just another chance to take pride in oneself,

You feel forever defeated because you judge thyself,
Then call me conceited, 'cause I love myself.

Maybe, One Day

I wish you could've known me;
When I knew what me was,
You could've loved me,
Like no one else does,

I wish you could've seen me,
At my highest heights,
I wish you could've heard me,
Laugh on the darkest nights,

I wish you could've known me,
When I was sweet and kind,
I wish you would've loved me,
But no, never mind.

Cinema

Almost no one makes my heart feel full,
Almost no one can make the two halves, whole,
Almost no one makes bad days seem not dull,
Almost no one has a beautiful soul;

Except for you,

Someone to make everything better with,
No one I'd rather get breakfast with,
No one I'd rather be messy with,
No one I'd rather grow old 'n' play checkers
with,

Few things rival her intelligence,
Only her elegance, and benevolence,

If she meets diversity, she has endless
prevalence,

She is as perfect as can be,
Breathtaking, truly a cinema, a movie.

Redecorate

To see her as I see her, you'd need a new
eyepiece,
She's as my favorite showpiece,
I hope, one day, her heart, I can appease,
With the hope that our wallets will be obese,
She's a creator, everything she's made, a
masterpiece,
She's my queen, my chess piece,
Conquering my enemies and granting me peace,
She's the only one I'd give my heart up for
sub-lease,
If I were to redecorate, she'd be my centerpiece.

Outlook

Shed a tear from missing you,
So sad, I brought my whiskey too,
All my nightmares have come true,
My entire mood is killed without you,
My days are mediocre, save when I'm with you,
I don't feel sober, I'm no longer a floater,
She put the drive in my motor,
When everything was all astray,
With my feelings, she's never played,
When I'm with her, I'm better than okay.

Companion

With me through my highs and my lows,
Companionship knocks, and friendship grows,
With me through laughter and tears I've shed,
Always by my side, where our dreams are bred,

Moments we share, my spirit soars,
Your dear companionship is worth so much
more,
Hand and paw, we walk this path together,
Through sunny, or stormy weather.

Anchor

Life's waters are deep, where currents play,
Our Anchors rest, in a lucid bay,
As the oceans begin to stir,
Its steady grip holds me, safe and secure,

Steel arms grip, a steadfast hold,
Keeping me safe, and keeping me bold,
Storms rage, and tempests roar,
The Anchor keeps me chained to the shore,

I constantly test this device,
Anchoring myself, to be precise,
In times of trial and in times of glee,
My Anchor keeps me rock steady.

Drown

Words are like waves, crashing down,
In complete silence, you can still drown,
Metaphoric tons, the anchors weigh,
Dragging down the light of day,

Sinking beneath the weight of thought,
In the constant darkness, my battles are fought,
The currents drag me deep,
To the depths, for me secrets to keep,

But from the depths I rise,
Breaking through the watery guise,
My words transform, now wings to soar,
From the drowning depths, to the distant shore.

Reminisce

In the halls of our head, memories reside,
Like a woven web, a constant flow of time,
Sparkling like diamonds, in time's endless
stream,
Every moment a delight, a loitering dream,

Threads of our soul, wound so tight,
Guiding us onward, through darkness, and
through light,
Though time may fade them, they never truly
die,
Yes, memories always linger, they never say
goodbye.

Descent

A soft breeze grants a leaf flight,
Fluttering down, flickering through the softest
lights,
Golden rays paint the autumn air,
A leaf makes its descent, without a care,

From soaring heights to the earth's embrace,
In its quick journey, it found its place,
A fleeting moment, yet so profound,
As the cycle of life, continues 'round,

I've learned from this humble leaf,
That in letting go, there is beauty beneath,
Even in descent, life shows us art,
That we can always keep close to our heart.

Paper

I am like paper,

I fold under pressure,
I crack from the heat,
I wilt from the cold,
I tear from the force,

I am like paper,

In my folds, tales unwind,
A blank canvas for an open mind,
In libraries vast, I've found a home,
In books where wisdom's seeds are grown,

I am like paper,

So thin, yet strong and true,

Paper binds words for the whole world to view,
Paper binds us in unknown ways,
A vessel for everything, come whatever may.

Hurdle

In life's great game, hurdles we face,
Yet through the struggle, we find our place,
With hope in heart and strength in soul,
We'll rise above, and reach our goal,

Every step forward helps overcome fear,
We find our strength, holding back the tears,
The hurdle isn't just about winning the race,
It's about the journey itself, and each challenge
we face.

Outcast

A different soul, in a world so huge,
Where fitting in is only a ruse,
Misunderstood, yet fiercely you,
They see the world in a unique hue,

So let the world pass you by,
In solitude's haven, spread your wings and fly,
For at the height of solitary skies,
You'll discover that strength never dies.

Renewal

Intoxicating as a daydream,
Making things not as they seem,
Soothing me from my worst extreme,
Making everything fly in my bloodstream,

Forever keeping me humble,
Without it, I'd fall and stumble,
All my cookies would crumble,
Feeling like a bee, without its bumble,

I thought my heart might've died,
Until the day you graced my eyes,
I wish to always be by your side,
You're captivating personified.

Loss

In the quiet hush of a gloomy night,
Where my fears linger, devoid of light,
They echo a whisper, dreary and slow,
A lament for the one I've had to let go,

I cherish some moments we've shared,
In love's embrace, this loss can't be repaired,
Loss is a heavy weight upon my fragile frame,
My scars are unseen, but etched all the same.

Fantasy

In a realm where dragons soar high,
A wizard chants beneath the sky,
In a castle tall, with towers bright,
Where stars coat the blackest night,

Enchanted lands where dreams take flight,
Magic weaves through day and night,
Wishes whispered in the breeze,
Bringing forth adventures and tales to seize,

In fantasy's embrace, I find a release,
Where all of my problems seem to cease,
Every page, a world anew,
In fantasy, my dreams can come true.

Shatter

Glass shatters, a symphony of pain,
A moment of loss, but also of bitter gain,
Hopes fracture, memories dissolve,
In fragmented pieces of what we can't resolve,

Yet from the wreckage, we gleam,
A chance to mend our shattered dreams,
For in the broken, is a chance to rise,
A rebuild, beneath the brightly lit sky,

So let the pieces fall where they lay,
In a shattered state of disarray,
From the scraps you can find,
A stronger you, redefined.

Self-War

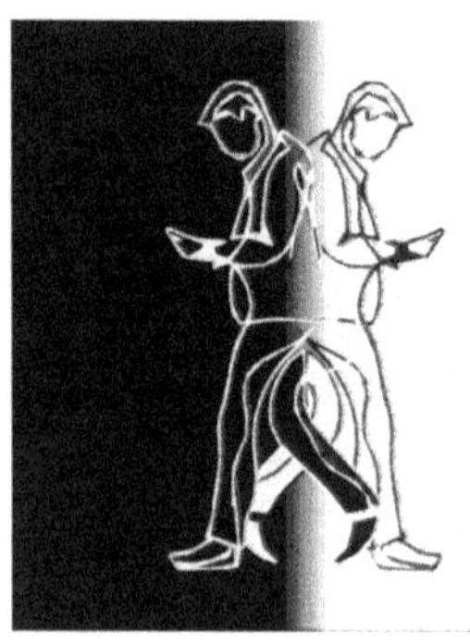

In the trenches of my brain, a fierce fight,
A battle waged in the dead of night,
Two of me clash, in a raging storm,
One seeking solace, one seeking a new form,

Doubts set sail, the arrows fly,
Courage stands, watching with a steadfast eye,
Fear and hope, they forever contend,
In the labyrinth where my thoughts descend,

But amidst the chaos, a truth unfolds,
In every struggle, my story unfolds,
For in a battle within one's mind,
Means the strongest you survives.

Unspoken

You can say a lot,
By doing a little,
Spewing food for thought,
But the words seem so brittle,

Muted dreams, like challenges unseen,
Dance within my silent scene,
Yet in the silence, a power grows,
Casting long dark shadows,

My words would be regal,
The first of their kind,
For the quietest people,
Have the loudest minds.

Encouragement

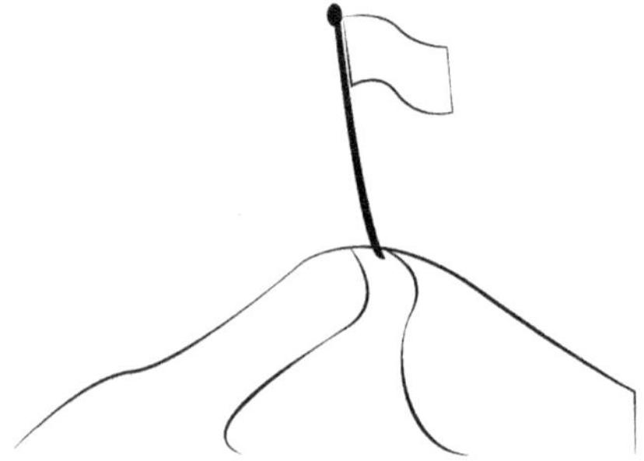

In the grand race of life, when paths seem
unclear,
Courage booms loudly, banishing fear,
Each step taken, doubt disappears,
For in my heart, I know, victory is near,

So I lift my chin and stand tall,
For in every stumble, there is a call,
To rise again, and give your all,
With courage strong, you'll never fall,

Believe in you, and what you do,
The world's waiting, it's up to you,
Embrace each struggle, see it through,
For encouragement will guide you true.

Unclear

A maze of uncertainty, where paths emerge,
A whisper slings doubt, and a booming urge,
Questions linger, like shadows on a long day,
Casting doubts, but also taking them away,

In the realm of unknown, fears may reside,
Confusion reigns, on this bumpy ride,
Each step taken, with trembling feet,
Uncertainty's grip, feels so sweet,

Embrace the uncertainty, with open arms,
For within its grip, lie unseen charms,
In life, uncertainty roams,
But keep faith and courage, you'll always find
home.

Ego

Ego reigns supreme,
A never ending stream,
An arrogant stride,
A relentless tide,

A fancy gait,
A deadly fate,
A gentle cure,
An overwhelming allure,

Ego reigns high,
Beneath the sky,
With head held tall,
So eager, ready to fall.

Solitude

In the silence of my solitude, my heart dwells,
Where my words falter, my emotions swell,
Misunderstood is my soul,
A feeling that takes an unforgiving toll,

Misunderstood gestures, misunderstood cries,
In the depths of solitude, my soul dies.

Scream

I've always felt unheard,
Trapped in a cage, chirping like a bird,
Just trying to find the right word,
But you just think I'm absurd,

I'm chirping louder, fiercer,
A growing scream, an ear-piercer,

I can't take it anymore,
This repetition became a chore,
This schedule became a bore,
One that would eat me at my core,

This is why I scream.

Delinquent

I hate it.

I don't care.
I don't care that the mitochondria is the
powerhouse of the cell,
Sitting in here is like waking through hell,
What's the difference between a classroom and a
jail cell?

I already know how to spell,
I just want to yell,
Or maybe, fall down the stairwell,
I can't wait to hear this goddamn bell,

I hate it.

Unbreakable

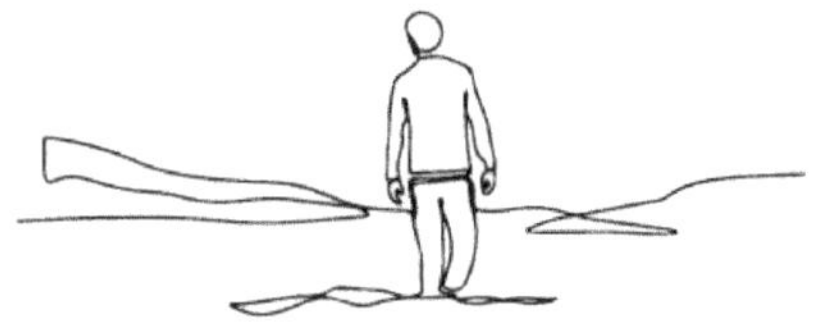

I'm a mighty oak, rooted deep into the ground,
I've weathered tempests, terrifying, profound,
In every storm, I stand tall, unshakable,
Through thunder and lightning, I'm unbreakable,

A heart of steel, a spirit, unbound,
On the darkest nights, my purpose is found,
The world throws it punches, its blows,
I rise, forever taller, my roots only grow,

I'm a mighty oak, in the face of a gale,
Through winter, and through hale,
My roots never fail,
Unbreakable, I prevail.

Brushstrokes

Conformity all around, I stand alone,
A unique creation, only I've known,
For in my differences, I've found my worth,
An orchestra of individuality, echoing my
rebirth,

I am the brushstroke in an artist's tale,
Painting me in a massive scale,
Every stroke, forging my path,
Embracing my soul, unmasked,

Colors splash on this canvas wide,
Each soul shines bright, within its own stride,
In a world of strokes, each one sleek,
Individuality is what makes them unique.

Ghost

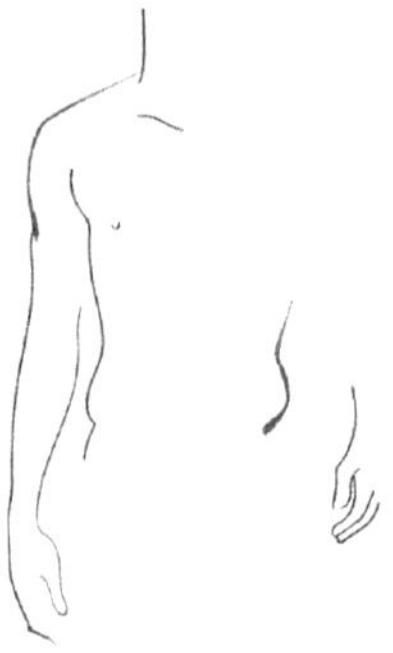

I am here, but you do not see me,
Not in a cell, but I don't feel free,
I am felt, but not seen,
A phantom of your past, serene,

A guardian of secrets, everything you adore,
In a deadly perdition, forevermore,
A guardian of memories, lost and found,
I can scream, but I won't make a sound,

Heed my silent plea,
Cherish everything, set your soul free,
For I am your haunting host,
Still wishing you the most.

Silence

Silence can be calming
Silence can be unnerving,
Silence can be everything you desire,
Silence can be a horrific amplifier,

Silence can be fantastic,
Silence can be drastic,
Silence can be the worst,
Silence can be the best.

Chains

A constant drift, afloat in the mind,
Strengthening its grip, holding me in its bind,
I've held it in high regard, even enshrined,
In turn, it's left me blind,

It dragged me down, I fell behind,
My health, my aspirations, my world, declined,
Like a serpent, it coiled tight,
Constricting joy, consuming all my fight,

It starts with whispers, soft and low,
A tempting call, that will always grow,
It feeds on dreams, thrives on pain,
Leaving only resentment in its stain,

Love, support and might,
Breaking those chains, reclaiming my fight,
For in the heart, there is a unique key,
Used to break the chains of addiction's tyranny.

Everest

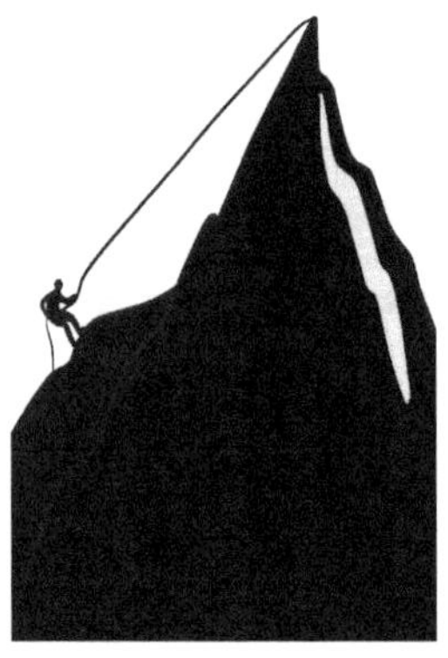

I am climbing to the mountain's peak,
You haven't even tried,
You said, "nah, it's too steep,"
My journey will leave you wide-eyed,

The sky kisses my cheek,
A moment you'll forever seek,
The air is thin, the wind, fierce and wild,
Yet my determination is undefiled,

Here's to the climbers, bold and brave,
Keep going, you'll reach the peak you crave,
In your quest for the peak, you'll find your
worth,
A testament of your strength, and your soul's
birth.

Craving

Like my favorite food I'll always crave,
I know I'll take this feeling to my grave,
I don't even remember how to behave,
So grateful, because my soul, she's saved,

I've never been in such a rave,
The last decade, I've lived in a cave,
Digging my own six-foot grave,
Like time's little slave

I no longer find the need to dig,
My heart has never been this big.

Goldmine

Sometimes when I'm fine, I'm not really fine,
Sometimes I whine, when I'm really fine,
Sometimes, I get really out of line,
But, there is someone who puts me on cloud
nine,

She's my favorite morning headline,
Her presence, simply divine,
Perfection in design,
I knew I struck the goldmine,

When I was able to call her mine.

Phoenix

In ashes born the phoenix flies,
Through sunlit skies, it boldly glides,
With feathers blazing, it soars above,
A symbol of eternal love.

From flames she rose, fierce and free,
A beacon of hope, for all to see,
In every trial, she finds her strength,
Defying fate, going to any length,

Any thought easy to discern,
For in her heart, a fire burns,
A lesson learned, as time yearns,
A glorious rebirth, she's assuredly earned.

Life

A quiet whisper is dawn's embrace,
Where morning dew adorns each bug's face,
Beneath the canopy of a blue,
Where dreams and hopes breakthrough,

Through ravines deep and skyscrapers tall,
In every heart, lies a beckoning call,
To wander through the realm unseen,
And grasp at any truth that lies between,

In each moment, our universe unfurls,
A mosaic of life, a string of pearls,
For within each full breath,
Lies the essence of life, defying death.

Facade

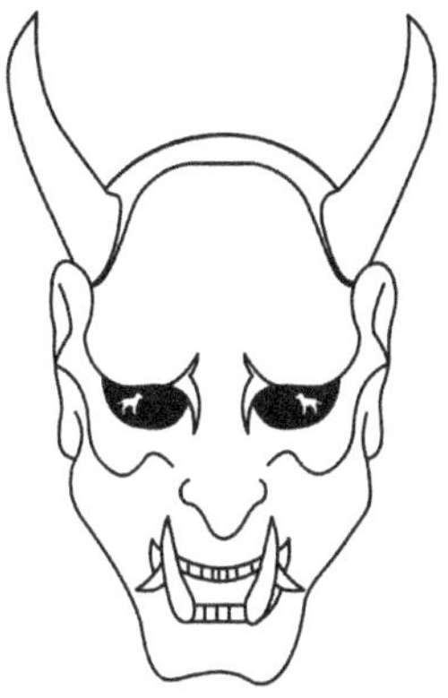

Thin is the veil I wear,
Concealing truths that my soul laid bare,
Behind my mask, a silent plea,
It shields my heart, but also sets me free,

I fashioned this shield of a woven guise,
To brave any storm, to soar the highest in the
sky,
Yet the mask, serves another role,
To hide my essence, to guard my soul,

In veiling truth I lose my sight,
In seeking refuge, I shun my light,
Peel away my layers thin,
You'll see my beauty held within.

Material

Wealth, glitter and gold,
Where trinkets are brought, and trinkets are sold,
But material treasures are fleeting and vain,
They'll swiftly fill a soul, then swiftly leave in
pain,

In the grasp of possessions, we often lose sight,
Of the true riches, found in pure daylight,
For in bonds that bind, and moments that're
shared,
Lies a real wealth that cannot be compared,

Cherish what is real, beyond what we own,
Within love and connection, true riches are
grown,
Treasure each other, in life's awkward
procession,
We walk along, guided by our hearts, our prized
possession.

Grind

Hustling and bustling drive the working day,
Tasks and deadlines pave our way,
From dawn's first light till the evening's call,
We labor on, working until we fall,

In the rhythm of work, a routine is found,
A melody of purpose, echoing oh so profound,
During the day of work, we truly come alive,
Filled with passion and dedication, we thrive.

Dance

The cusp of the arena, where warriors stand,
All weapons drawn, ready for command,
Their movements fluid, a daring chance,
Each tempting strike, a deadly dance.

Swords and shields clash in a rhythm of chimes,
The fighters move to the beat, always on time,
With grace and skill, they weave and sway,
In their fierce dance of melee.

Each parry, each thrust, a mesmerizing sight,
The dance of battle takes all the night,
With valor and honor on their heart,
Both warriors playing their part.

In the dance of battle, they've shown their
might,
A testament to courage, strength, plight,
They honor each other, in valorous stance,
In the humble dance of battle's advance.

Regret

My heart aches, I breathe a heavy sigh,
Regretting choices that have passed me by,
In the depths of hindsight's bitter gaze,
Despair lingers in my somber maze,

A shadow cast upon my soul,
As memories of mistakes take their toll,
Chances lost, now forsaken,
I can only ponder the paths I could've taken.

The Ants

In the world so vast, lies a kingdom small, yet
quaint,
Within it lives a tiny ant, a diligent saint,
Legs swift and impossible to toil,
Across the grass they tirelessly roil,

In lines it marches, with a purpose clear,
Gathering crumbs, exploring with no fear,
A tiny adventurer in a vast domain,
Fearful of every droplet of summer rain.

With comrades in arms, they build their nest,
A fortress strong, filled with zest,
Each grain of sand, each leaf they haul,
In unity, their motivation calls.

Ledge

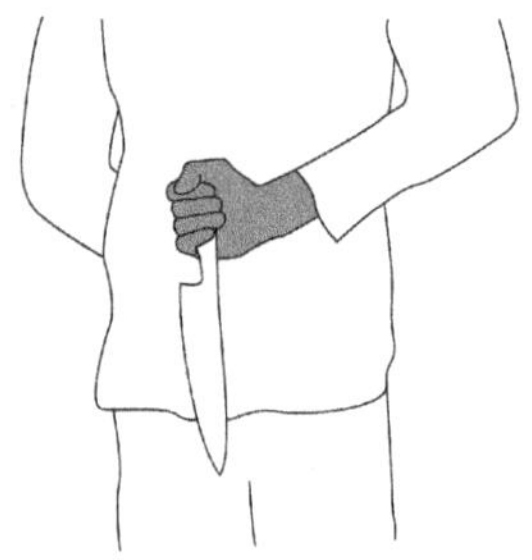

Upon the ledge we stood, my friend and I,
With laughter and spirits soaring high,
But, a playful jest to one, a gentle shove,
And suddenly I fell, fell, from above.

The wind rushes by, a blur of blue sky,
As I fall down, I cannot help thinking, "But why?",
My heart races, anxiety grips tight,
In this moment, full of spite,

Trust I thought we shared,
But our friendship was just ensnared,
I descend low,
Betrayal's fall, a bitter blow.

Desire

In life, desires unfold,
Dreams come to life in stories told,
It's through climbing mountains, not just slopes,
To get what you want, it takes more than hope.

Every step, the vision grows more clear,
Passion ignites and doubts disappear,
The universe hears, the steps align,
Destiny weaves its intricate design.

Getting what you want is not an easy feat,
It's about perseverance, through cold and heat,
Sweat and tears, an undertaking grind,
The resilience to keep pushing, deep in mind.

Getting what you want is more than gain,
It's about growth, it's about pain.
It's about discovering what you're made of, and
realizing you are enough.

Failure

Shadows stretch and daylight fades,
Failure casts its dreadful shades,
Not defeat, not your end,
A chance to rise, to mend.

So embrace the stumble, the erring stride,
For in failure leads the journey's greatest guide,
It leads us to heights we've yet to know,
Where we'll rise, taller, stronger, as we grow.

The Hunt

Bow in hand, and ready,
Moving with purpose, slow and steady,
Tracking prey through brush and thorn,
The quest of the hunt, where stories are born.

The rustle of leaves, the whisper of trees,
Guides the practiced hunter with ease,
Silent steps, relying on eyesight keen,
In the heart of nature, a primal scene.

The thrill of the chase, adrenaline surges,
As the hunter and the hunted merges,
Through misty mornings and golden light,
They chase the wild, the hunter's plight.

Island

Alone I stand, an island in the sea,
Surrounded by waves, in vast obscurity,
The ocean's embrace, a solitary shroud,
As I wander the shores, feeling unbowed,

I am both king and slave,
A sovereign ruler of my own enclave,
With every passing tide, I feel the weight,
Isolation's burden, a heavy freight,

The ocean's song is my company,
As I stand alone, ever free,
For on the shores of my isle,
I find a sanctuary, to dream and smile.

City Street

Cars pass, painting a picture of blurring motion,
Horns blare, adding to the commotion,
People weave through the bustling crowd,
A whirlwind of souls, walking proud,

Street performers add to the cacophony,
With music and dance, they create a harmony,
Children laugh and play without care,
Amidst the chaos, a moment oh so rare,

Every corner, stories to be told,
On a busy street, where life unfolds,
A basket of life, woven with care,
This busy street holds magic in the air.

Naive

In the garden of naivety, I roam,
Innocence blossoms, unburdened by gloam,
With eyes wide open, yet not fully aware,
I wander through life, without a single care,

Trusting blindly, with an open heart,
I stumble through this world, playing my part,
Unaware of deception, in ignorance's sway,
I dance to melodies, not knowing their disarray,

In the garden of naivety, I take my place,
A child of wonder, one of a fleeting race,
Innocence falters, illusions fade,
In the garden of naivety, where my memories are
made.

Other Half

Love's embrace, where the hearts converge as
one,
I find my solace in your tender gaze,
With every breath, our melody has begun,
A symphony of passion in love's haze.

Your touch, a gentle breeze that stirs my soul,
Igniting flames that dance in blazing heat,
In your embrace, I find my sweetest goal,
Where our essence and our power meet.

Let us dance, two souls forever entwined,
In love's sweet symphony, our hearts aligned.